EVERY ANGLER'S GUIDE TO

AMAZING

LURES AND FLIES

EVERY ANGLER'S GUIDE TO

AMAZING
LURES AND FLIES

*Rare and Forgotten
Masterpieces of Fishing*

DICKSON SCHNEIDER

VIKING

Many thanks to Dawn, Tiffany, and Samone.
As well as to David Stanford, Lorraine Kisly, and Richard Whittaker.
Also thanks to my dad who told me all those wild fishing stories.

VIKING
Published by the Penguin Group
Penguin Books USA Inc., 375 Hudson Street, New York, New York 10014, U.S.A.
Penguin Books Ltd, 27 Wrights Lane, London W8 5TZ, England
Penguin Books Australia Ltd, Ringwood, Victoria, Australia
Penguin Books Canada Ltd, 10 Alcorn Avenue, Toronto, Ontario, Canada M4V 3B2
Penguin Books (N.Z.) Ltd, 182-190 Wairau Road, Auckland 10, New Zealand

Penguin Books Ltd, Registered Offices: Harmondsworth, Middlesex, England

First published in 1997 by Viking Penguin, a division of Penguin Books USA Inc.

1 3 5 7 9 10 8 6 4 2

LIBRARY OF CONGRESS CATALOGING-IN-PUBLICATION DATA
Schneider, Dickson.
Every angler's guide to amazing lures and flies : rare and forgotten
masterpieces of fishing / Dickson Schneider.
p. cm.
ISBN 0-670-87512-0 (alk. paper)
1. Fishing lures. 2. Flies, Artificial. I. Title.
SH449.S33 1997
688.7'912—dc20   96-38124

This book is printed on acid-free paper.

♾

Printed in Singapore
Set in Monotype Walbaum
DESIGNED BY BRIAN MULLIGAN

PREFACE

I have spent much of my life pondering the relationship between humans and fish. Although I've enjoyed fish and fishing since I was a child, my serious fascination with the subject began in the late 1970s, when, as a graduate student, I assisted a group of Austrian engineers who were working on problems of hook design. One of their findings was striking.

A human brain is on average fifty times larger than a fish brain. But humans use only five percent of their brains, while fish use 100 percent of theirs. Professor Karl von Hammerstadt of the University of Vienna first discovered this while studying trout in the Alsace region of France. A fish has a total brain power of 2 vH (von Hammerstadts). A human has 2.5 vH.*

As these figures clearly indicate, the average human is only 25 percent smarter than a fish. I think this explains a lot.

—Dickson Schneider

---

*Certainly there are exceptions: Einstein had 3.9 vH—and was, by the way, an excellent fisherman.

INTRODUCTION

Water always seems so full of promise. We find ourselves staring into a rainy gutter, watching ripples. We look down into a stream, a pond, a lake—from deep within a fish is calling. The quest to catch this fish is one of our most ancient desires and doubtless the source of one of the first human rituals, fishing. Over time fishing has developed into a kind of interspecies communication, evolving to a level of complexity where the men and women who pursue fish share certain of their experiences.

For one thing, the great fishing lures and flies have all caught fishermen before they caught fish. Each time we stroll down the aisle at the local sporting goods store each of us ponders the same questions: Do I need another Flammo lure—perhaps the really big one, the two-ouncer with the purple dots? Does the #14 Palmered Crotchfly actually lure big brownies out of deep holes?

It should come as no surprise to know that lure manufacturers have studied fishermen as intensely as fishermen study fish. The Gordon Company in 1908 hired a full-time "psychosis" (years before the term "psychologist" became the appropriate professional moniker)—not to study fish but to examine the reactions of fishermen to different lure designs. In fact, the founders of the first two television advertising agencies both started out as bass lure design consultants. As early as the 1930s researchers using hidden cameras filmed bass fishermen and recorded their pupil responses while observing new lures. These remarkably entertaining films feature a split screen. On the left a lure comes into view while the researcher announces its name ("Lunker rama 950" or "Yellow Bass Blaster"). On the right is a close-up of the fisherman's pupil—opening wide in an obvious Pavlovian response.

Decades of research and experimentation have combined with the folk wisdom and ingenuity of the traditional angler-craftsmen to give modern angling an astonishing variety of bass lures. The success of the Lure of the Month Club, the rapid proliferation of the Bass Web on the Internet, and the crosscultural fertilization of the World Bass Movement confirm that the evolution of the bass lure is far from over.

The dissemination of fly patterns has been much more haphazard, since so many trout fishermen tie their own flies. The vehicle is almost always a great name, such as the Olive Dakota. Fantastic stories as to its effectiveness are attached to the name, along with a vague description of the fly, such as "an olive hackle yellow tinsel body turkey fan wing." Soon five hundred versions of the fly, none alike, have appeared throughout the country, and fishermen correspond, congratulating one another on the potency of the fly—while in fact each is catching fish on a unique variation.

Photography and the color printing of magazines and books changed this distribution pattern, yet not as thoroughly as one might assume. The fly tyer is fiercely independent. Though the intent may be to copy a particular fly precisely, invariably the design will be "improved" by the tyer. Thus, for instance, it is almost impossible to find two identical examples of the legendary Ignatz fly—drawn by cartoonist-outsdoorman George Herriman in the 1930s—despite the fact that it appeared nationwide in the funny pages on the same Sunday. Most anglers claimed they had difficulty finding the correct brick-red hackle feathers, a weak excuse at best.

Over the years a heated rivalry, or at least a seasoned enmity, has developed between bass fishermen and trout fishermen. Many bass fishermen have privately expressed to me their concerns about any activity performed in rubber pants. While trout fishermen tell me the bass anglers just don't get it —fly fishing is a *civilized* sport. For those of us who take a broader view, the artistry and intelligence behind all fishing lures is the same, but to simplify matters for the reader we will separate the book into two sections: Bass Lures and Trout Flies.*

*Obviously those who would pursue any fish using "bait" do not deserve further mention.

BASS LURES

M ost people do not realize that Large- and Smallmouth bass, re-
lated species, are native to the Nile River in Egypt, where they
grow to an average size of only twelve inches. They were inadvertently
imported to the United States in 1630 when a barrel of drinking water
containing bass eggs was dumped from a ship into what is now known
as the James River in Virginia. The fish thrived, rapid evolution in the
new environment increased their size enormously, and they became an
important food for the early colonists. In 1641 a famine struck
Jamestown, and the settlers endured "Bass Winter" surviving on only
bass and berries for over six months.

Teddy Roosevelt commissioned the first national study of bass in
1903—he himself was not a bass fisherman, but his wife was obsessed
with it. This study, conducted by the Biology Department at Harvard at
a cost of almost $16,000, identified all potential bass habitats in North
America. Trainloads of bass were subsequently dispatched throughout
the entire continent.

The creation of bass lures (also called plugs, jigs, or crankbait) was a
direct result of the introduction of efficient, mechanically advanced

reels in the late nineteenth century. As the equipment became mass produced and widely available, the novelty and excitement of fishing with artificial lures quickly caught on. "Bass fever" swept the country, and the lure industry took off. By 1923 bass fishing was rated second only to baseball as a national pastime. Since then its popularity has diminished slightly (though Half-Bassed, found in bar tables throughout the South in the mid-1970s, was one of the most popular of the early computer games), but the legacy of the great bass lures is by now a vast and fascinating body of work. In presenting the following examples—a small sampling of the thousands of lures that have been created—it's helpful to point out that bass lures generally can be divided into three categories: clown lures, stealth lures, and scientific lures.

An effective clown lure can make a bass more agitated than a couple of sinners in the first pew. Clown lures operate on the theory that if you get a bass mad enough eventually the enraged creature is bound to strike. It'll jump right into your tackle box, and it might bite your dog as well.

Stealth lures address the opposite side of the fish's personality. Bass are smart—anybody who's spent six hours hauling weeds out of a pond knows this. Stealth lures try to sneak by, and this insults the fish. Bass don't like to be made the fool, and nothing drives them crazier than to see an outsider slowly creeping through their territory.

Scientific lures are based on one of several principles: sonic tones, neutronics, bimodal impulses, to name a few. Much of the scientific exploration is inspired by folklore—the entire study of noise-making lures came from the old Florida tradition of banging a tambourine against the side of the boat while rowing back and forth across the lake. The lore was that it awakened the fish. The science proved it.

MIDNIGHT RAMBLER

{ 1927 }

I t's just a jointed, spoon-faced, floating diver, but on that fine Georgia spring day in 1927 it was the resurrected savior and all the apostles to Jack "Bacon" Freeman. Using this lure he caught the three largest bass ever taken at the Macon "Bass-steal Day" Festival. The biggest of the fish, nicknamed Jack, Jr., mounted and waxed, is still proudly displayed over the front door of the family restaurant in Savannah. The Rambler hangs from his upper lip.

CRAZY BOOG

A lot of these were sold, and they influenced popper design considerably. A simple, colorful, noisy, and effective lure, it was named by the inventor's cousin, the well-known Delta bluesman Eddie "Fishhead" Wilson.

THE UGLY STICK

{ ca. 1910 }

I found this in my uncle's garage in south Texas. He told me that my great grandfather made a lot of them. The old man just used a stick, a can of fence paint, and a couple of hooks. He even put a spinner on this one. He said the bent stick made it move in the water "like a broke grasshopper." My uncle always used store-bought lures and was happy to bequeath me this heirloom.

DARWIN'S LOGIC
{ 1925 }

There is nothing subtle about this lure. The first one was carved and assembled by a reporter covering the Scopes Monkey Trial in Dayton, Tennessee, in 1925. Big fish eats little fish—will the lunker come out to conquer? Another reporter was working on an equally impressive lure called Chicken and Egg, but was unable to decide on the final arrangement and, confounded, threw it in the trash before it was finished.

JUNIOR DUCK

{ 1959 }

You won't find this in the Fisher-Price catalog, although you should. My father made this for me when I was three. With my one-piece, forty-inch closed-face Zebco starter set, I did all right. Who can forget that first bass? It was less than a pound and Dad said it looked embarrassed for taking this lure. I kissed it and we let it go.

GORDON #6

A classic lure from the Gordon Company, which dominated the bass lure industry for over a decade. "The Company," as fishermen called the firm, was always in the vanguard of bass research. In the years before it developed neutronics and other technical approaches, the firm produced numerous lures with propellers and other gadgets. This one is a basic floating-clown-torpedo, and it caught a lot of fish in its day.

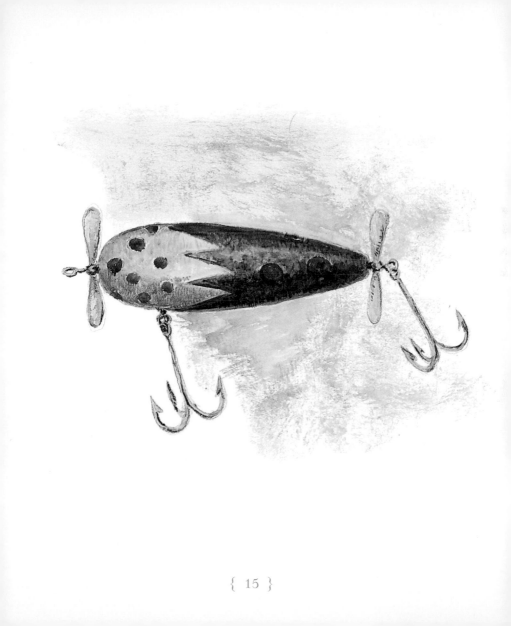

BAKELITE™ BASS-BEACON
{ 1939 }

The Bakelite™ Bass-Beacon was prominent in the "New World of Plastics" pavilion at the 1939 World's Fair in New York City. The display included a three-hundred-thousand-gallon plexiglass tank filled with Largemouth bass. A mechanical arm jibed a hookless Bass-Beacon through the water while observers watched the bass strike the lure again and again.

BABY RATTLE
{ 1955 }

This lure was built using an actual baby rattle—one of the early experiments with "noise plugs." Subsequent research into sound led to more effective examples. This lure did attract fish, but they were usually undersized.

Steel-Plated
Lunker Lure

T his is a very rare handmade lure. A Louisiana sheet-metal worker named Mr. Ouija made these cork-bodied, steel-plated babies out in the workshop behind his house. He apparently tested his lures right from the back porch of his shop, which faced the bayou. People swore they worked, and a few were sold at the local bait shop. This lure, the only surviving sample of his craft, is too fragile to test in battle, so we can only speculate about its effectiveness.

LITTLE RED MOUSE

In the thirties every tackle box had a felt mouse in it, though it's not clear why. A few bass were caught on these, but usually by accident—this lure was fabulously unsuccessful. How often do you see a mouse make a break for it across a lake or a pond? Mice *walk around* large bodies of water. For a brief time the Gordon Company offered a version that let you attach a small piece of actual cheese to the spoon. But to purists this reeked of "bait fishing," and the lure was quickly discontinued.

CHOPPER LURE

A fter seeing *Easy Rider*, a Florida lawyer claiming to be a professional bass fisherman managed to raise a million dollars from
retirees and had these lures manufactured in Costa Rica. For a few
months they were distributed nationally through truck stops, but the
investor, along with over $500,000, disappeared. Quite rare and valu-
able to collectors today, the lure actually caught a surprising number of
bass.

FARNEY BUZZER

Anton Farney, pioneer aviator, avid fisherman, and part-time scientist, was smitten with the sublime motion of a propeller moving through liquid. He felt certain that fish would share his fascination if this movement was brought to their attention correctly. This lure is one of the last of a long series he produced in over sixty years of investigation into the efficacy of propeller lures. Unfortunately, Farney never found the exact combination of propellers needed to catch fish, and when he died at age eighty-nine his research was abandoned.

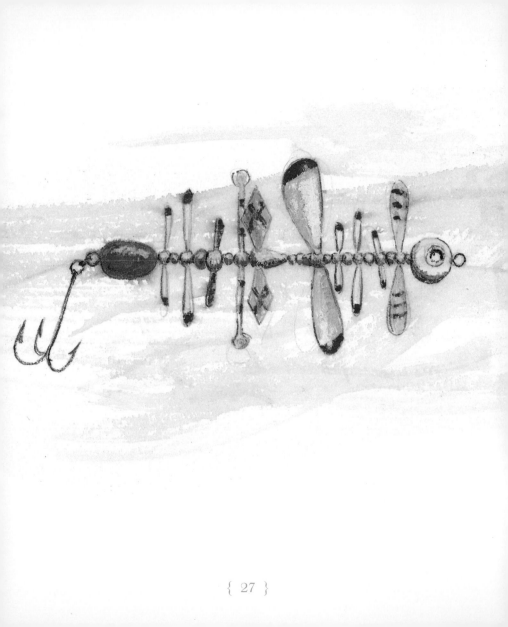

WOODY

D uring World War II it was nearly impossible to get new paint in
the United States. Naturally this shortage didn't stop resource-
ful fishermen. This lure's hardware was salvaged from other lures and
applied to a hand-carved walnut body. Paint from dwindling prewar
supplies was used sparingly, and the whole thing was dipped in
lacquer.

THE HOLMSTROM
INCREDO-POPPER
{ 1966 version }

The very small Holmstrom Fishing Lure Company (1932–1969) was operated by three brothers from a Quonset hut in Elk River, Minnesota. For thirty-seven years they manufactured only this one lure, the Incredo-Popper. The only variations over the years were in color—if you have the 1941 green-and-white, you are a wealthy fisherman. A great lure for getting the bass riled up on sluggish days, it featured a four-inch aluminum popper in front, and the noise it made could wake a dog after a three-day hunt.

Neutronic Cicada

This was the first neutronic lure ever produced—note the telltale ridges on the side, which should produce the neutronic effect. For some reason this lure was not popular, and only a few were sold. When the manufacturer, the beloved Gordon Company, went out of business during the Great Depression, all of their research on neutronics was lost.

CANDY CANE
{ 1957 }

The large hook made the Candy Cane tough to use in a weedy pond, but this 1957 lure was a good one. A little jig on the line made the propeller spin, the skirt dance, and the whole thing dive toward the bottom. For years this was a popular stocking stuffer.

FISH FOOD

I found a whole box of these at a yard sale in Missouri for two dollars. The seller said his daddy used to own a Happy Gas station in Louisiana, right after World War II, when the gas wars began. They were already practically giving the gas away when the promotions started: steak knives, dishes, whirlygigs for the car antenna. A Happy Gas Fish Food lure was free with a fill-up. At first the lure was a big hit, but patrons started coming back with the classic complaint: "Didn't catch nothin' . . ."

POKE POLE DEMON

{ 1932 }

This was all the rage in the thirties down in Florida. You put about four feet of strong line (at least thirty-pound test) on the end of a ten-foot pole. You sneak up to the edge of the water and drop this monster into a hole in the weeds. Just a little wiggle and it splashes around like crazy. Some people caught big bass on these things, but there were skeptics. "Whatever you catch," they'd say, "poke-poling isn't fishing."

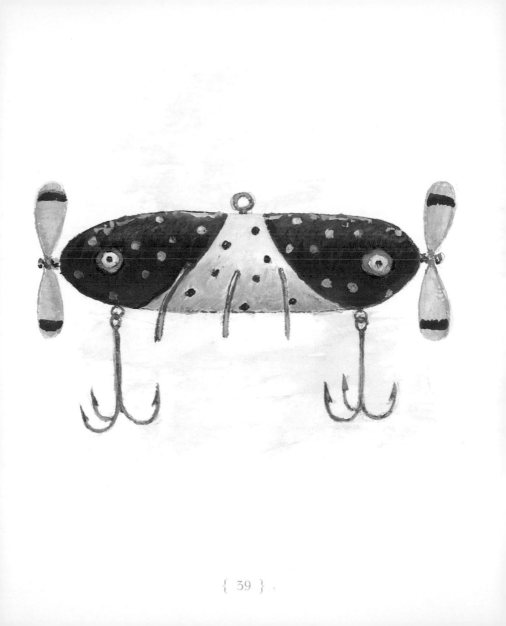

TOLEDO TORPEDO

Max Waxman, who ran Waxman's Bait Shop in Toledo, designed this lure, and he paid a local orphanage to make fifty. The lure has a painted cork body, and a wire through the middle connects the line and the steel hook. The first customers came back raving over the lure, lugging buckets of bass. Waxman raised the price from a nickel to a quarter, borrowed some money, and ordered another three thousand. But this second batch proved entirely disappointing—no one caught anything. Waxman lost his shirt, and his mind. For the next five years, passersby would spot Waxman each morning, summer or winter, hopelessly casting the useless Torpedo into the Maumee River. He died a broken and befuddled man.

Years later, research confirmed that Waxman had stumbled upon the phenomenon of electrolics. The original set of lures had used copper wire to connect the hook and line, which happened to create the "electrolic effect"—irresistable emanations of electric current produced as molecules of copper (diode) are deposited on the steel (anode). Waxman's second batch of lures had used a steel wire to connect the hook and line, thus destroying the lure's effectiveness.

ELECTROLIC BOMBER

{ 1924 }

T he electrolic effect, discovered by Waxman, was finally identified and explored in 1923 by Professor Edward Humbert, a consultant to the Gordon Company. They quickly created a popular line of electrolic lures, which included this one. The copper and zinc electrodes protruding from its sides created a virtual vortex of electrolic vibration through the water. Unfortunately for anglers in the South, this lure attracted not only bass but also quite-agitated cottonmouth moccasins. It was immediately banned in several states, and, in an overreaction fed by the sensational silent film *Snake Madness,* which, incidentally, was produced by the Gordon Company's chief rival, Dudley Sharpe, Ltd., all electrolic technology was prohibited under federal law in 1928.

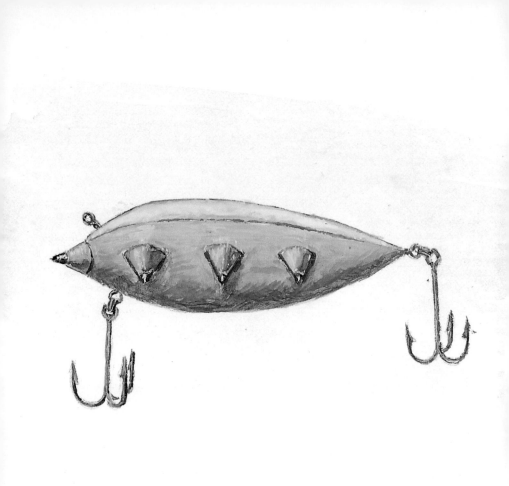

In the late 1920s the Gordon Company hired several designers from the avant-garde Bauhaus school, hoping to incorporate modern ideas into lure design. The following two lures were created during what proved to be a brief, and not yet fully understood, period of innovation.

FISH CUBES
{ 1928 }

P ablo Picasso's influence on lure design cannot be understated. This Picasso-inspired popper has eight eyes on one side and six noses on the other. The hope was that the bass would believe he was swallowing a whole school of minnows when he hit this lure. Like most of the early modern designs it was ahead of its time and failed to catch many fish.

CALDER'S CARP KILLER

{ 1929 }

A lexander Calder himself designed this extraordinary bass lure (the name was just a joke). Only two hundred were made, so this is quite a collectible. George Wilson, owner of Freddie's Bait and Beer in Lawrence, Kansas, found a carton of twelve in the store's basement in 1974 and began selling them for $2.50. A local art history student recognized the lure and alerted Wilson, who was able to sell the rest to museums and collectors. The last one went at auction for $48,000.

T R O U T   F L I E S

Decorating a hook (or angle, from the Anglo-Saxon *ongle*) with feathers and other materials in order to attract fish has been an art form for centuries. The first English-language fishing book, *Treatyse of Fyshinge with an Angle,* by Wynkyn de Worde (believed to be a pseudonym), was published in 1496. It begins appropriately, "Thaet Fyshinge befloes frome the beste of noable desyres, thaet the Fyshe, and the Spoart, and the flote of the flye upon cleayre Watere and the Angler, toagether muste yet feyl a tastee of Paradyse." Who can argue with that?

Although at least one species of trout is native to nearly every body of cold water on the planet, anglers have also helped to transport their favorite species worldwide. As human populaions moved they also brought their fly-tying skills with them, and in some instances history can be traced by the movement of designs—as with the sudden appearance of the infamous Turkish Harhar flies in seventeenth-century England.

Countless great flies and fly-tying techniques have no doubt been completely lost to us. Others are remembered only by vague descriptions in obscure texts. An example is the mysterious purple Trout Howdy fly

Faulkner mentions in his notes. But with such a stunning array of flies that have been passed down generation to generation, and with striking advances in both technique and approach in our own century, we need hardly dwell on our losses. What follows is merely a sampling of the work of a truly vast tribe of fly-tyers.

THE HATCH

"Match the hatch! Match the hatch!" This is the mantra of the trout fisherman. Early in the morning one often finds the trout voraciously breakfasting on a cloud of insects hovering just above the water. Close inspection reveals the "hatch" is a group of insects so tiny that offering your smallest #24 fly to them is like casting the Titanic into a sea of rowboats.

Here we see three very common insects—all are essential to the trout diet, yet all are essentially mysterious. Entomologists have yet to observe them in any other stage of development or anywhere else in the ecosystem except hovering over the water. They seem to exist only as trout food.

CADDIUM   IN DOOFUS   IXNAY
SPECULUS   IN FINITESIMUS   EEUM SAY

MIDGE FLIES

These tiny flies will give the fly fisherman some hope of catching fish during a hatch of very small insects. Technically, all flies tied using hooks size 26 and smaller are "midge flies." Some fishermen have gone so far as to use microscopes to forge special #36 hooks in order to create flies only one-sixteenth of an inch long. These are unbelievably difficult to tie, and one is lucky to get even the vaguest resemblance to an actual insect. On the other hand, trout don't have magnifying glasses, so midge flies can actually be very effective if conditions are right.

DETAIL

HOUSE FLY

In 1874 in the northern California logging town of McKinleyville, an English emigrant named Byron made a barroom boast that he could catch a steelhead with any kind of gear, using any lure or fly. Another gentleman pulled this House Fly out of his pocket and bet a hundred dollars that Byron was wrong, challenging him to use it on a twenty-foot bamboo pole with two feet of line. Amid great laughter, the red-faced Englishman accepted the bet.

The next morning found Byron knee deep in the Mad River, clumsily swishing the House Fly in the water. In less than a minute, with remarkable luck, he caught a four-pound steelhead.

Every year on the second Saturday in December, "Byron's Bet" is celebrated with an enthusiastic re-creation of the event—several hundred anglers gather and wade forth with ungainly rigs and House Fly versions. No one since Byron has ever caught a single fish, yet the event gains in popularity every year. Beer is a factor.

PINK POODLE

I n 1954 two movie producers in Palm Springs were lounging by the pool, talking about fishing. They got to bragging about their fly-tying skills, and eventually it got to the point where one of them wagered that he could catch trout using a design based on his dog Noodles. The rest is history. Made of dyed virgin-wool balls and feathers from a flamingo, this "puppy" will float all day. The proud owner of the original speculates "trout must think it's prom night for mayflies when they spy this tumbling down a riffle."

HACKLE JACKAL

{ date unknown }

O riginally tied as a hat decoration, this fly resembles no living thing. Almost useless for fishing, it always looks spiffy on a homburg.

PRETTY BABY

{ 1924 }

S ome flies, such as this one, are simply beautiful. To cast such a fly and see it float downstream is a kind of ecstasy. Some fish recognize beauty and in a fit of bliss will hammer such a fly. Anglers swear the fish will look them in the eye in that supreme instant.

This fly, by the Welsh tyer responsible for the memorable World War I flies Dogfight and Spad, is a classic example from the Aesthetic Era of British Fly Tying (1920–1927). During this period fly shows were as popular and well-attended as cricket matches. Flies were judged in equal parts for their technical construction, effectiveness, and beauty.

THE BOTTLEBRUSH
{ 1948 }

If you think something about this fly says "Mexico," you are right. It mimics the Mezcalito caterpillar of the Sierra Madre. But its origins are American—Bogart himself tied this fly in a bar at 4:00 A.M. and used it at sun-up to skunk John Huston in a fish-off. In fairness it should be said that Huston was drunk and using a shotgun. But the fly has subsequently earned its reputation as a fish charmer.

HALLEY'S COMET
{ 1910 }

H alley's Comet generated worldwide interest—and a certain degree of panic. The arc of the comet passing overhead suggested this streamer to a New England fisherman-astronomer. He made and sold several hundred using the slogan, "This too shall pass!" Halley's Comet wasn't the end of the world, and the fly quickly disappeared, but it may make a comeback.

Hudson Meadow Moth

{ 1921 }

C ontrary to common assumption, this fly has nothing to do with either the Hudson River in New York or the car. Hudson Meadow is actually a lake about fifteen miles from Ketchum, Idaho—its name an attempt by locals to conceal a prime fishing spot, known for its abundance of large native trout.

Hemingway wrote of this fly in his diaries: "Fished with the Meadow Moth today, kept six fine trout. Goddamn, it's a good fly. A man can take this fly and fish with it."

REDWING BLACKBUG

{ 1964 }

This western fly is patterned after a rare insect found in the Idaho panhandle. One word of advice—if you are using the Blackbug during a hatch, wear some repellent. They bite like hell.

SIBERIAN HUGE FLY

T rout are usually viewed as gentle, wily, and essentially harmless creatures, especially compared to aggressive fish like the Largemouth bass. However, the Giant Siberian Lake Trout (which can weigh as much as 350 pounds) is regarded as the most dangerous creature in freshwater, more dangerous than even the Nile crocodile. Feeding mostly on frogs, birds, raccoons, and carp, this fish has been reported to leap thirty feet out of the water to snatch a mallard in full flight.

Special steel fly rods and heavy wire leaders are required to pursue this vicious fighter, as well as great strength and stamina. The fisherman must be able to cast the enormous twenty-five-inch-long yak hair streamers that have proven so effective with these giants. It is quite an experience to watch this fishing: the loud "Whomp! . . . Whoosh! . . . Whomp!" of the fly rod, the surprisingly gentle landing of the streamer in the water, and the truly frightening strike of the fish make the Siberian an unforgettable adversary.

We have featured here a half-scale section of the business end of one of the streamers. The only other fly that has ever been used for this fish was one made with a stuffed sixteen-inch coot. Known to locals as The Big Dead Duck, no example has survived.

Nonsymmetrical Caddis

T he theory of nonsymmetrics is based on the idea that a fly can represent an insect *in motion*. Usually, as in this example, the rear portion will mimic a real insect tail, while the front will present a jumble of contrasting elements. Although the theory seemed promising, it was not really pursued after World War II.

SPECKLED SPIDER
{ 1940 }

Another of the few surviving nonsymmetrics, this was a great "fly." The protruding peacock hurls waved crazily in the current. Many fish were caught with spiders, although, due to the delicate construction, an individual specimen could only handle a few trophies before it was ruined. Somewhat more durable was a smaller, simpler version known as "Itsy Bitsy."

SILVER BUG
{ 1934 }

For over sixty years the Silver Bug has been known to only one person—"Larry," of Pinedale, Wyoming. He ties five different sizes of this extraordinary dry fly, which he swears will consistently bring reluctant trout out of the depths, even if the water is murky after a storm. "Larry" said the burden of concealing this fly was too much for him, and he's also having some heart trouble, so he asked me to include it in this book so it would not be lost to the world. Our examination of the fly indicates that it produces a weak but steady neutronic effect. The secret is *real silver wire* wound around the thin cork body. Enough said. Try it. And give a tip o' the rod to "Larry."

TRENCH FLIES

Every student of World War I knows that for the soldiers in the trenches, life on the Western Front was a nightmare. It's less well known that one of their primary joys was the vast amount of time they devoted to tying flies. As one trench poet wrote in a letter home, "This fly I tie / Yet before the dawn / May it see me with a trout back in Wolverhampton." Clearly the art form helped dispel both boredom and the horror of war.

Clubs arose, tying competitions were held, and the effects, not only on morale but on the art of fly-tying, were remarkable. Actual fishing or even casting was almost impossible—an untimely competition held around a flooded shell crater at Ypres led to the deaths of over thirty anglers. Fly designs became more abstract, less concerned with mimicking insects. Historians cite this as the beginning of the era of Modern Fly Tying—one of the world-changing consequences of the Great War.

WOLLY FITZROY #8
{ ca. 1914—1918 }

Many of the most accomplished of the World War I fly-tyers were British. The Wolly Fitzroy was named after a famous staff sergeant of the Third Grenadiers. More precisely, it was named after his moustache.

QUAD NYMPH #12

The Quad Nymph was designed by an artilleryman who was struck by the beauty of the first four-bladed propeller airplane to see action in Europe—the De Havilland DHXIII, less gracefully referred to as "the Tinbelly." Vigilantly keeping watch for these flying beauties, he created this fly as an expression of his love.

BRIGHTON FURBALL #14

{ca. 1914—1918}

For decades after the war, merely saying the phrase "Brighton Furball" would automatically bring peals of laughter at any gathering of veterans. As feathers became scarce on the front, innovative materials were incorporated into designs. This ball of lint, wherever it came from, makes a very convincing fly.

LOVEJOY'S RED CROSS

{ 1917 }

J ames Lovejoy, an avid fisherman and sportswriter in civilian life,
tied this fly in his hospital bed in Paris in gratitude for the driver
who had rushed him from the front. In his memoirs, written when he
was fifty, he claimed the heroic driver had been none other than Hemingway. In his later years he changed his story and said it had actually
been Harry Crosby. The true story proved far more mundane, even for-
gettable. But the fly endures.

THE KAISER
{ 1917 }

T he yellow belly and the white streak down the back of this streamer tell the story—this is clearly the commentary of an American.

CAPTAIN WINSLOW'S
RED-EYE GRUB #6

{ 1917 }

Captain Winslow tied the Red-Eye Grub immediately after returning from a harrowing all-night recon mission. Indispensable to the creation of this landmark fly is the complex and difficult double-overhand-back-hackle knot. Caught in no-man's land by a massive barrage, Winslow lay pinned to the mud for hours, stunned and terrified. Suddenly a vision of this knot appeared to him. He clung to the image for hours, until he could make his way back to the trenches, whereupon he quickly captured the vision in filament form. Winslow lost most of his hearing in the ordeal but always said it was a price well worth paying for so elegant a knot.

BLOODY HELL— AKA WITCH'S BREW

{ 1918 }

A nother British fly from World War I, this one has been a dynamo in the streams of Scotland ever since. Created during the Second Battle of the Marne, it came to be regarded as a kind of memorial to all the fly fishermen lost during the Great War. To be authentic, the body must be made with a thin strip of old boot leather—or a rat tail —wrapped in black chenille and the red hackle. Part nymph, part streamer, part dry fly—it can be fished in three ways.

In San Francisco during the early fifties fly fishing was an important part of the Beat scene. Widespread interest in Buddhism and nature naturally led to Zen Flies. It was admittedly a passing phenomenon—as one angler-poet later explained in City Lights Review: "It got to where 'the perfect cast' meant 'no cast.' Eventually we just went swimming." Influences from the Zen Fly period can be traced on into the sixties. For example, the lyric "Fly Jefferson Airplane" was taken from a fishing poem by Richard Brautigan. Then there is the lettering carved deeply into a cliff above Muir Beach: "First there was a fish, then there was no fish, then there was." But of course the primary and most eloquent record is the remarkable flies (we have included four examples here) that have made their way into the hands of collectors over the years.

ZEN BUG
{ 1953 }

I found this one-of-a-kind fly in a Salvation Army shop in Hollister in the early seventies. It was glued into a little wooden box with the following words hand-lettered on the inside of the lid:

> zen bug sits
> cool
> go fish

ZEN BUG

ROADKILL
{ 1955 }

This Beat fly is made simply of squirrel hair embedded in asphalt. It floats about six inches under the water and looks like a dead caddis nymph. A journal entry suggests it was created from a gob of Interstate 5 on an oven-hot July day near Redding by poet Lew Welch, who was stranded while hitchhiking to Mount Shasta.

THE FLY OF ONE HAIR
{ 1955 }

Although it was tied in San Francisco in 1955, this legendary fly has been kept in a monastery in Japan since 1963. It consists of a single strand of Buddha's hair wound around a hook. The black, seven-inch hair was noticed by poet Gary Snyder on the back of a dog that wandered into Vesuvio's, the North Beach coffee house.

THE HOOKLESS HOOK
{ 1956 }

This fly has taken many a patient angler off the deep end. The Hookless Hook was meant to catch a "spirit fish." As an anonymous twelfth-century Chinese poet wrote: "A fish that can be caught with the hookless hook can likely guide us through the gateless gate. And then who is caught—the fisherman or the fish?"

SECRET WEAPONS

D uring the long history of fishing, lures and flies have come and gone. They disappear for one of three main reasons.

1) They looked good but didn't work (the most common reason).
2) They worked but were not popular because of some aesthetic prejudice or whimsy of the marketplace.
3) They worked too well and have been banned.

There is only one example of the third case—The Lure and The Fly. Developed by the Gordon Company, these two designs are such powerful fish attractors that they would inevitably clean out any body of water. Even if you catch and release, the same fish will hit them again and again until they die of exhaustion and perforation.

What is the secret? We couldn't tell you even if we knew, but apparently the principle is the same in both The Lure and The Fly and is allegedly something remarkably simple. We interviewed the last surviving person with direct knowledge of the devices—Walt Brisbane, who worked in the mailroom at the Gordon Company in 1914 when these were being tested. He remembers that the tests were "more like a trip to a fish market than to a stream. The largest fish fought each other to get at them."

The Gordon Company, realizing their devastating potential, never released the designs. By presidential decree, the company was granted the only nonmilitary secret patent ever awarded by the United States. They were never given market names and will be forever known simply as The Lure and The Fly.

The following pages reveal the only drawings ever made of these devices. Portions have now been declassified—the parts which still cannot be shown are concealed. We offer them for public view as a caution, trusting that the knowledge that weapons of such awesome power exist will inspire us to be vigilant, so that both fish and humans will endure. Face it, we need each other.

THE LURE AND THE FLY

{ 1914 }